Twins-Duo Delight

Parenting Twins: Discovering the Tricks & Treats

Kavita (Mili) Jain

Dedication

I am deeply grateful to my husband, Mayank Jain, for being my steadfast companion on this journey. I would also like to express my sincere appreciation to my parents, as well as all the pivotal figures, teachers, and guruji who have blessed me with the ability to tread this path.

My late father, a beacon of inspiration, continues to watch over me from above, guiding my pen as I embark on this literary journey. Despite originating from a small conservative society, he motivated me to reach greater heights, and his memory remains a constant source of strength and inspiration.

I would like to extend a special acknowledgment to Dr. Madhuri Patil, a resilient guide, and "Inspiring Jatin," my motivational coach, whose belief and encouragement transformed my long-standing dream into reality within days. Thanks to them, I leave behind a meaningful "Legacy" for my children.

This book finds its roots in the inspiration provided by my twins, Stuti Jain and Darsh Jain. Their arrival has infused these pages with a profound meaning and purpose, ensuring that it will remain a lasting echo of my presence when I am no longer in this world.

3

Epigraph

"In the symphony of life, three hearts beat in one body—a harmonious dance of twins and mother, an unwritten tale of love that knows no end."

– *Kavita Jain*

Foreword

Darsh and Stuti, the fraternal twins, had an unbreakable bond. They were both incredibly creative and when they entered my classroom, they stuck to me like glue. It was as if they had known me since the beginning of time. I remember how tiny they were, but their personalities were larger than life. Darsh, especially, was very fond of me and wouldn't leave my side, even if I had to use the washroom. It was like he had his version of "Mary Had a Little Lamb" playing in his head. They were intelligent and excelled in their studies, but what stood out was their incredible artistic talent. The way they could draw and express themselves through art was remarkable. As their teacher, I grew incredibly fond of them, and even now, years later, we still keep in touch.

- Manju Bhandari, Twin of my sister, Teacher of Darsh and Stuti

Table of Contents

Introduction

Oh! The enchanting world of motherhood!

It's one of the greatest and most fulfilling gifts bestowed by Nature. You're cradling a tiny, delicate bundle of joy in your arms, and waves of tenderness overwhelm you when a tiny precious bundle of joy is placed into your waiting arms, and when it is placed double in the arms you've entered the realm of extreme parenting. Double the hugs, double the love, double the snuggles – it's a whole new level of joy. Of course, with the good comes a tad more challenge, just to keep things interesting.

Now, imagine being a mother of fraternal twins – a dynamic duo, one boy and one girl. Talk about a double whammy! Raising twins, they say, demands more time and effort than handling a solo act. People often throw the question my way, "How do you manage with two?" Well, these twins happen to be my first babies, so I'm dancing to the rhythm of the double beat from the start. I simply do it all twice – double the giggles, double the bedtime stories, and yes, double the midnight diaper changes.

And here I am, penning down my unique journey in this book, a journey that's a tapestry of memories woven with threads of amazement and wonder. It's not just a narrative; it's a treasure trove of tricks and treats, a guidebook that connects with every parent out there. Because, let's be honest, whether you're dealing with one bundle of joy or a duo of mischief-makers, the shared experience of parenthood is a rollercoaster ride we can all relate to.

As Ricki Lake wisely puts it, "Motherhood is the greatest thing and the hardest thing." Ain't that the truth? So, buckle up, fellow parents, as we embark on this joyous, challenging, and downright magical journey together. Get ready for a rollercoaster of emotions and a sprinkle of wisdom – because parenting, especially the double kind, is a wild ride worth savoring. Let the tales, tricks, and treats unfold!

Three Hearts in Unity!

Oh, the dance of three hearts in unity! Imagine it – not just one heartbeat, but the rhythmic symphony of three hearts pulsating in unison within a single body. Being a mother of twins isn't just a biological marvel; it's a canvas where the limits of the human body blend seamlessly with the expanses of the heart.

In this chapter, we dive deep into the incredible journey of carrying twins, where the physical and emotional boundaries are stretched beyond imagination. Picture this: the awareness of not one, but two precious lives flourishing within you. It's a sensation that goes beyond words, as your heart has multiplied, and now, in perfect harmony, three hearts beat in one body.

As we navigate this journey, we unravel the intricate dance between your body and the lives it nurtures. The heightened awareness of every little movement, the simultaneous flutters and kicks – your body becomes a vessel of life, pulsating with the energy of a triple heartbeat. It's a journey where the maternal bond takes center stage, an unspoken connection that transcends the ordinary. Your heart beats in synchrony with your twins, and an inexplicable sense of unity envelops you, fostering a love that knows no bounds.

Yet, amid overwhelming joy, the feeling of having twins isn't without its emotional nuances. We explore the highs of elation and wonder, as well as the occasional moments of doubt and apprehension. The weight of responsibility may feel heavier, and unexpected challenges may arise but fear not – the resilience of your heart will guide you through.

But here's the magic – within these pages, we share the intimate stories of mothers who've danced to the rhythm of three hearts. Their experiences offer glimpses into the depths of their hearts as they navigate the complexities of carrying and nurturing two lives within a single body. It's a journey that demands strength and resilience, yet each story reveals the immeasurable love that blossoms within them.

So, join us in this exploration of the indescribable feeling of having twins, where the symphony of three hearts beating as one creates a tapestry of love, strength, and extraordinary connection. Through these shared narratives, let's honor the profound experience of carrying twins and celebrate the awe-inspiring journey of motherhood.

What is it like for some parents to raise twins?

Boy! The rollercoaster ride of raising twins – overwhelming, exhausting, exciting, and amazing! Let me whisk you into the world of one parent who found themselves navigating the thrilling journey of twin parenthood.

Picture this: I was living in the United Kingdom, marveling at the bustling families with twins around me, but little did I know that soon, I'd be at the center of that whirlwind. The revelation of my twin pregnancy hit me like a  whirlwind – a bit late, but undeniably a double blessing from the heavens. The doctor's words, asking me to listen to the heartbeats of both Baby A and Baby B, left me bewildered. Excitement, tears, and nervousness about the impending responsibilities swirled within me.

As time marched on, the journey got tougher, but I clung to the belief that the challenges were merely stepping stones to something extraordinary. My uncle, a reassuring presence, reminded me that the pain would fade away once I held both my bundles of joy. Parenting is known to be demanding, and twins? Well, that's like turning up the difficulty level. Yet, despite the challenges, I was determined to focus on the positive aspects that made life with twins truly remarkable.

The day of the C-section brought nervousness, but the doctors, in a heart-warming twist, asked if I preferred twin girls or twin boys. My response was simple, "I want both." The magical words, "You got both," echoed in the room, and as the nurse placed each child on my left and right, I marveled at the perfection of this divine indication. A left-handed baby from my left womb and a right-handed baby from my right – a unique adventure indeed.

With this beautiful indication, my journey of raising twin blessings began. Each step was infused with memorable moments, a mix of tricks and treats, valuable lessons, and growth opportunities. And so, the incredible treasure hunt of parenthood unfolded, a journey where the overwhelming exhaustion was met with unparalleled joy, making every twist and turn worthwhile.

Balancing Gender and Individuality: Nurturing Twins of Different Genders

One of the most daunting tasks of my parenthood has been the delicate art of balancing gender and individuality in the enchanting world of fraternal twins— one girl and one boy. "Balancing Gender and Individuality" takes us on a delightful journey, exploring the unique challenges and joys that come with nurturing these two distinct individuals who share a special bond as siblings.

From the way they learn to talk to the outfits they do, every aspect unveils the nuanced dance between their differences and similarities. It's like watching two sides of a coin spin and twirl, each side reflecting its own unique story. The challenges and happy moments of raising these fraternal twins become a captivating narrative, a tale of discovery and growth that unfolds with each passing day.

In this chapter, we peek into the intricacies of parenting twins of different genders—their quirks, preferences, and the magic that happens when you strike the perfect balance between honoring their individuality and embracing their shared connection. How do you navigate the terrain of toys, interests, and personal spaces when you have a girl and a boy growing side by side?

As we explore the challenges, we also celebrate the joys—the laughter that fills the air, the moments of discovery when their unique personalities shine, and the beautiful harmony that emerges when you nurture the individual spirit of each child. It's a delicate dance, but one that adds layers of richness to the tapestry of parenthood.

So, join us in this exploration of "Balancing Gender and Individuality," where the canvas of raising fraternal twins is painted with vibrant hues of diversity, love, and the sheer magic of watching two unique souls blossom under the same roof.

Chapter 1: Embracing Their Differences

Understanding the importance of individuality in twins

In the captivating journey of raising fraternal twins, the first step is understanding the vital role of individuality. Every tiny detail, from characteristics to preferences

20

and talents, contributes to the unique identity of each twin. I vividly remember being mindful of these differences, steering clear of dressing my son in feminine attire for those playful photos. It's the little things that matter, creating an environment where each twin feels genuinely valued for their authentic selves.

Acknowledging and celebrating their gender differences

Fraternal twins – like any other siblings – bring a unique blend of tricks and tons of fun! They're not identical puzzle pieces; instead, think of them as a dynamic duo, each with its distinct shapes and colors. Celebrating what makes each twin special is the name of the game!

As they grow, fraternal twins unveil their personalities, interests, and talents, akin to having superhero sidekicks with their superpowers. Parents get the front-row seat to this fantastic show! Embracing the twin magic means cheering for their uniqueness instead of comparing. It's like having two favorite ice cream flavors – different, yet equally awesome!

Encouraging them to make choices, from picking superhero capes to deciding what game to play, fosters independence. It's about nurturing their super identities beyond being twins.

Navigating the galaxy of individuality within twins is akin to being the co-captain of a fantastic spaceship. Each twin becomes a distinct planet, full of quirks, surprises, and fun features. Picture one as the reserved stargazer and the other as the daring explorer, always ready for exciting escapades.

The adventure unfolds with one twin expressing creativity through colors and art, while the other passionately kick a football on the ground. Picture this cosmic scenario: while the mother takes a nap, a secret science experiment unfolds in the bathroom, and the faint aroma of something burning acts as a moving alarm clock, summoning you to witness the scientific genius in action. Yet, when hunger strikes, the kitchen becomes a culinary playground, turning your twins into gourmet chefs whipping up bagels, mug cakes, cheese balls, and occasionally a seven-course meal with a side order of kitchen chaos. Waking up to find your child evolving into an all-rounder eagerly awaiting applause for their talents adds a delightful twist to Mama's adventure. Amidst this endless exploration and shared adventures, a symphony of laughter and joy echoes eternally as you wake up to find your child evolving into an all-rounder eagerly awaiting applause for their talents.

Super Communication Skills

Great superheroes always communicate effectively. Establishing open communication within the family ensures everyone's voice is heard and valued, just like a superhero team meeting.

So, let's celebrate the fantastic adventure of having fraternal twins – the unique superheroes in the family!

Chapter 2: Language Development

Gender conscious Teaching language and communication skills

Oh, the enchanting journey of guiding newborns into the realm of language and communication! For a mother, it's a divine gift, but when you're raising fraternal twins, the challenge takes on a whole new dimension. Imagine attempting to teach gender-specific language simultaneously – English may provide a straightforward path, but when it comes to the mother tongue, the complexity deepens.

The twins found themselves entangled in the intricacies of gender-specific sentences, presenting a puzzle that required thoughtful consideration. After a fair bit of juggling and brainstorming, a strategic shift emerged as the solution. Teaching each twin separately became the name of the game – it's like sending them on personalized language adventures, untangling the gender-specific sentence puzzles.

This adjustment wasn't just a logistical move; it was a deliberate effort to untangle the confusion and pave the way for a smoother language-learning journey, one tailored to the unique understanding of each twin. The language classroom transformed into a space where individuality thrived, allowing each twin to grasp the intricacies at their own pace. It's a bit like crafting a customized roadmap for their linguistic exploration, ensuring that language development becomes a joyful adventure rather than a confusing maze.

So, here's to navigating the exciting twists and turns of language development with fraternal twins, where the magic lies in tailoring the journey to fit the unique nuances of each budding linguist.

Chapter 3: Clothing Choices

Ah, get ready for the most exhilarating part of the parent playbook – decking out your very own living dolls! And when the heavens bless you with fraternal twins, it's like rolling out the red carpet for a double-feature fashion show starring a mini princess and a dashing prince. Picture twirling crowns on one side and slipping into cute little coats with sweet bows on the other – a parade of frilly shoes to stunning boots, creating a delightful fashion spectacle. It was as if God handed me a canvas to paint a beautiful world of style and play.

The shopping sprees were nothing short of epic, transforming the wardrobe into a magical kingdom of fashion adventures. Every color under the sun made an appearance as we mastered the art of balancing gender neutrality and breaking away from gender stereotypes. Some outfits quickly became favorites, and the twins, in their tiny expressive ways, made it clear which ones they wanted to flaunt. Dressing up felt like creating a brand-new doll every day, capturing these moments in pics for the memory bank.

But here's the cardinal rule that guided my choices – no matching outfits for these individual wonders. They're not clones; they're unique souls, each with their style. And let me tell you, when they spot a twin-like outfit in photos, it's a hilarious discovery they enjoy to the fullest.

My go-to mantra for their wardrobe was simple: comfy equals calm, ensuring they stay serene for the long haul. Because in this fashion-forward adventure, comfort reigns supreme, making sure my mini fashionistas are ready for whatever the day may bring.

Chapter 4: Navigating Gender Expectations

Navigating the tricky waters of gender expectations – it's like setting sail on uncharted seas, challenging societal norms that often dictate how children should behave based on their gender. And when you're raising fraternal twins, the complexity of this journey takes center stage, especially when family stereotypes favor boys, potentially sidelining the girl child.

In my journey, I confronted this challenge head-on, determined to ensure equal opportunities for both of my children. Reflecting on my childhood, I remembered how my father defied gender stereotypes, encouraging my sisters and me to explore activities traditionally reserved for boys. As a parent now, I fully comprehend the significance of the stance my father took for his daughters in those times.

He never imposed limitations, granting us the freedom to try anything a boy in the family could do, all while emphasizing the importance of discipline and boundaries. The goal is clear – to foster a mindset where a girl can be just as fearless and capable as her male counterparts. This transformative journey seeks to dismantle societal expectations, empowering children to chart their paths based on their unique interests, skills, and dreams, rather than conforming to outdated norms.

Imagine this journey as a vibrant playground, where every child gets to swing as high, climb as far, and dream as big as their heart desires. It's a journey of breaking down walls and creating a space where children can thrive on their terms, unrestricted by limiting gender expectations. Together, let's sail into a world where the possibilities are endless, and every child is free to be their authentic, extraordinary self.

Chapter 5: Education and Extracurricular Activities

Embarking on the educational and extracurricular adventure for twins is almost as complex as finding a life partner. Parents, like, face the challenge of choosing the right school and environment that caters to each twin's unique needs. It goes beyond academics; it's an emotional journey as well. Selecting a play school or nursery involves a deep trust in care and the yearning for teachers who feel like an extension of the family.

I distinctly recall peeking through the gate's hole during their first month of play school, despite the teacher's reassuring words. Choosing the right environment, teachers, and staff becomes a crucial task, setting the foundation for their educational journey.

As they progressed into the nursery, a stroke of luck blessed us with a class teacher who happened to be a twin herself. Half of my relief rested on her understanding, and her advice proved to be golden – keeping them in the same section. This strategic decision not only built confidence but also fostered support between them. A decade later, they still find themselves in the same section, navigating the delicate balance of sibling rivalry and deep bonding. Despite spending most of their time together, their interests and talents have diverged beautifully – one leaning towards the scientific realm, the other dancing to the rhythm of art. And that, my friends, is perfectly splendid to watch every single day!

I ardently believe in the importance of siblings attending the same school and, if possible, being in the same class. The sense of togetherness fostered by being in the same educational space creates a bond that lasts a lifetime. In a world where relationships, even with friends, can seem fleeting, maintaining this deep connection becomes even more precious. Despite the challenges posed by the current trend of shuffling students each year, I continue to champion the idea that keeping siblings together in school nurtures a profound connection and unity that positively influences their relationship in the long run.

Chapter 6: Supporting Sibling Bonding

Hmmm, the intricate puzzle of sibling rivalry, especially when your twins are in fierce competition due to being the same age. It's a tricky ride, presenting challenges for every parent out there. While some siblings strike gold and become the best of buddies, it's not uncommon for brothers and sisters to engage in epic battles. Witnessing these showdowns can be frustrating and perplexing, to say the least.

Most twins, like superheroes, have a dash of jealousy or competition thrown into the mix. Blame it on changing needs, unique temperaments, or the desire for special attention—whatever the reason, arguments, and bickering are on the menu. It's like trying to juggle a bunch of superhero powers at once!

Now, when the little superheroes start their arguments, the parental instinct might be to swoop in and save the day. But beware—too much intervention can lead to a whole new set of challenges. Kids might start expecting rescue instead of learning to tackle problems independently. It's like being caught in a superhero loop!

I made the mistake of intervening too much, creating an expectation that a parent would always come to the rescue. When one twin gets corrected, they might feel a bit insecure, thinking the other twin is getting more support. It's like accidentally revealing a superhero's secret identity!

So, the best strategy is to give them some space for a little while and then talk to them separately and calmly. It's like giving superheroes a chance to regroup before the next adventure.

Setting ground rules for acceptable behavior is superhero-worthy. Let the kids know that not everything in life will always be fair and equal, just like in the superhero universe. I tried so hard to make everything balanced and fair, but life doesn't always follow the superhero rulebook.

For instance, if one twin excels in one field and needs more time to experiment, the other might feel left out. Celebrating their progress openly is like announcing the winners of a superhero contest.

One superhero move that worked for me was sending them out to a nearby place or mall together. It's like a superhero mission where both learn a sense of responsibility. With some money in their pockets for shopping, it becomes a treat to discuss and buy the right things, be together, and look out for each other's safety. Sure, it doesn't always go smoothly, and you might get a call saying they can't tolerate each other's behavior, but sometimes things work with a bit of trick, treats, and maybe a threat or two. Building a superhero team (your family) comes with its share of pros and cons, but in the end, you're all superheroes in it together!

Managing the challenges of raising twins, especially when it involves "Balancing Gender and Individuality: Nurturing Twins of Different Genders," is like navigating through uncertain waters, similar to the mysterious Bermuda Triangle. It often feels like our efforts might disappear without a trace. However, the key to success in this intricate journey is to embrace the idea of restarting—a resilient and strategic approach that opens up new possibilities and guides us towards achieving a balanced and harmonious parenting experience.

Handling Parental Expectations and Self-Care

Sailing the seas of parenthood – a journey that not only brings the joys of watching your children grow but also presents the challenge of managing your expectations. As parents, our instinct is to wish for the best for our children yet finding that sweet spot between dreams and reality is crucial for nurturing a positive parent-child relationship.

In this intricate dance of parenting, it's crucial to carve out time for individual pursuits, ensuring that the noble task of parenting doesn't become a burdensome weight. Balancing time and responsibilities are not just important; it's a continuous learning experience. The inaugural step in effective parenting involves acknowledging personal expectations.

Living our lives and nurturing our kids simultaneously isn't an overnight accomplishment. It's a process that takes time to simplify, but it's achievable. There will be moments when kids demand all your time and attention, and that's perfectly fine. However, the next step is crucial to working on yourself. I learned this invaluable lesson during my parenting journey, and today, I happily share this golden rule: prioritize self-time and self-care.

One smart trick, passed down by my aunt with twin boys, is synchronizing their schedules. Making them sleep and wake up at the same time might seem firm, but it's a discipline that benefits both parents and kids. A decade later, the rule still stands strong, except on days when illness intervenes.

Practicing self-care is non-negotiable for effective parenting. Prioritizing your well-being equips you to handle the demands of parenthood while maintaining a healthy work-life balance. This balance is an ongoing journey, marked by trial and error. Remember, perfection is an unrealistic goal, and the parenting adventure is enriched by failures, growth, learning, and adapting to the ever-evolving dynamics of parenthood.

Parenting Strategies: Tailoring Approaches for Fraternal Twins

Encouraging Independence and Connection: Nurturing Individuality in Twins

1. *Building Outside Connections:*

   - ∞ Encourage twins to cultivate friendships independently of each other.
   - ∞ Foster a sense of independence by allowing them to form connections outside the twin bond.

2. *Celebrating Uniqueness:*

   - ∞ Emphasize and celebrate the individual differences between twins.
   - ∞ Create an environment that not only accepts but revels in their distinct personalities.

3. *Small Wins Rewards:*

   - ∞ Introduce rewards for small achievements to boost their confidence.
   - ∞ Make them feel valued and appreciated for their accomplishments.

4. *Family Teamwork for a Cause:*

> ∞ Encourage collaboration at home for meaningful projects and social services.
>
> ∞ Teach the importance of teamwork, responsibility, and giving back to the community.

5. *Individual Bonding Dates:*

> ∞ Establish one-on-one time with each twin for open communication and bonding.
>
> ∞ Treat them to personalized experiences, like a preferred coffee and a double chocolate chip Frappuccino date with the son and a shopping trip with the daughter to explore the current trend. This strengthens the parent-child connection individually.

6. *Surprises for Emotional Connection:*

> ∞ Incorporate surprises, big or small, to enhance emotional bonding.
>
> ∞ Provide gestures that make them feel cherished and connected, fostering a positive and loving atmosphere.

7. *Collaborative Art and Community Engagement:*

- ∞ Involve them in collaborative art activities and take up a stall in community events. This is not for money but for the sense of responsibility and understanding the efforts behind every penny.
- ∞ Teach the value of effort, responsibility, and using their resources to contribute to a cause.

8. *Family Traditions and Responsibilities:*

- ∞ Engage twins in family traditions, emphasizing the importance of rituals.
- ∞ Assign responsibilities like decorating for festivals and serving guests, instilling a sense of cultural appreciation and duty.

Encouraging independence while maintaining a strong familial connection is essential for the holistic development of each twin. These practices not only build their individuality but also strengthen their bonds within the family and the broader community.

Symphony of Fatherhood

It's like stepping into a dream. It is surreal. The day they came into this world, and I held them close, I didn't realize it was not just about them being born; it was my magical journey into becoming a dad. Two tiny wonders, fitting snugly in my palms, a bit light on the scale, and a suspicion of jaundice to keep us on our toes. With my little girl in the NICU and her mom on complete bedrest, I earned the exclusive ticket to visit her every few hours for the next two days. Every time she looked at me, it was as if I held the magic wand of protection, and our super special father-daughter bond just kept getting stronger with each passing year.

Let's jump ahead to the kindergarten chronicles. Initially, I stood sentinel outside the classroom with their mom. But, as luck would have it, they caught the usual bug that befalls every kiddo stepping into the wide world. I recall the day when dengue threw my daughter's fever into unimaginable heights, or the heart-stopping moment when she took a tumble from the swing, and we faced the unstoppable river of blood from a 4-year-old. Then, there was the time my son got a little too close to Diwali crackers burning his hand, and the day he had a not-so-smooth landing off his bicycle.

As a dad, I'd like to think I always wore the superhero mask, but underneath, tears were rolling down my heart whenever my little ones were in pain. That's just how the story of life goes, isn't it?

Now, let me share some key moments that have painted the canvas of our family tale, predominantly for father-centric domains in conventional households:

1. *The first party – learning to socialize:*

   The first grand party organized by their grandparents in our hometown marked a major milestone – their first birthday. It was no ordinary celebration; over 200 people gathered to share in the joy. Initially, we were a tad worried. Our little ones had never been amidst such a large gathering, and we feared it might overwhelm them.

   To our surprise, it turned out to be quite the opposite. The twins reveled in being the center of attention, surrounded by the affection and warmth of so many loving souls. It was heartening to witness, and from that day on, we made a conscious decision to expose them continuously to our extended family – a network of brothers and sisters, aunts and uncles, friends, and relatives.

   As family weddings and get-togethers became a regular affair, we noticed something remarkable. We no longer had to worry about where they were or how they were coping. The early exposure to diverse social settings paid off, and it became evident that our twins were growing up to be comfortable around different people.

Now, as they step into their teen years, I can see the dividends of those early decisions. They navigate social setups with ease, enjoying the company of family and friends. The once seemingly overwhelming gatherings have become familiar and enjoyable spaces for them.

In the grand narrative of raising twins, this chapter has been a testament to the importance of weaving them into the fabric of our extended family. The initial birthday bash served as a launching pad, propelling them into a world of connections and relationships that have enriched their lives. It's a journey that continues, and as a father, witnessing their ease in social situations brings a sense of fulfillment and reassurance.

2. *First long vacation – learning to plan:*

Our first long vacation happened when my twins were eight. Excitement buzzed through the house as we geared up for the adventure. We soaked ourselves into a shopping spree, making sure we covered everything on our list. The kids were involved in the process, of getting things of their choice. It was a great opportunity for them to learn about the things we buy from the market, how we negotiate, and how we plan our days. Even though they were too young to decide what was right or necessary, it was important to let them feel a sense of ownership.

Packing day arrived, and the twins were handed the responsibility of packing for themselves. From the morning ritual of brushing their teeth to the cozy routine of getting into pajamas before sleeping, they soaked in the details of our daily lives, which was their first lesson in planning their chores.

As we ventured into the unknown, the vacation turned into a whirlwind of experiences. The setting changed, and new characters emerged in the form of fellow travelers we met along the way. Each passing day was filled with laughter, surprises, and the occasional challenge.

Then came the moment of pure joy and connection. It was a sunny day, and we entered the adventure theme park. The kids, their faces lit with delight, raced towards the water adventure. As a family, we stood in the wave pool, did the water slides, and let the sun heat us. It was a snapshot of happiness etched into our memory.

As the vacation ended, there was a mix of nostalgia and satisfaction. We had navigated through the highs and lows of our journey, and the twins had not only discovered new places but also a bit more about themselves. The conclusion of this experience marked the beginning of a lifelong journey, filled with more adventures and lessons.

Looking back, that first long vacation wasn't just a break from routine; it was a canvas where we painted memories, and the strokes were colored with love, laughter, and the sheer joy of experiencing life together as a family.

3. *Illnesses and injuries – learning emotional strength:*

Navigating through illnesses and injuries with my twins became a defining part of my journey as a father. It's a delicate balance – the child seeks comfort, usually finding solace in the arms of their mother. Yet, there's a need for someone in control, to ensure that nothing goes awry. In our family, that was me – the father.

These moments were trying. Emotions ran high, and amidst the cries and occasional chaos, I strived to maintain a balanced view. As a dad, it was crucial to offer full empathy while providing calculated and well-understood responses. The sound often exceeded the pain, and in those moments, I aimed to be the steady anchor.

I recognized the importance of displaying emotional strength and being in control during these times. It was more than just a show; it was a genuine effort to assure my twins that everything would be okay. It wasn't about downplaying the severity of the situation but about being a pillar of support.

One instance that stands out is when, against the norm, I managed to get the personal mobile number of a well-known pediatrician from a top hospital. This ensured we could consult him anytime we needed. It might seem unconventional, but it was a testament to the lengths a father would go to for the well-being of his children.

These were not just episodes of sickness and injury; they were moments that shaped our family dynamics. Amid doctor visits, medications, and comforting hugs, I learned the true essence of fatherhood. It was about more than just being there; it was about being a source of strength, a provider of reassurance, and a constant in the face of uncertainty.

As the journey through illnesses and injuries unfolded, there were undoubtedly tough times, but there were also moments of resilience and bonding. We emerged stronger as a family, knowing that in the face of adversity, we could rely on each other. These experiences were threads woven into the fabric of our familial tapestry, creating a narrative of love, care, and unwavering support.

4. *First fight – learning resilience and courage:*

I vividly recall the first fight my twins had, and it's etched in our family history like a chapter in a book. A friend dropped by with his son, who turned out to be a bit of a mischief-maker. Now, my son, being the ever-nice host, was trying his best to keep things smooth.

But then, things took a turn. The visiting kid, probably fueled by some mischievous energy, started hitting my son, and that's when the tears started flowing. The whole incident was crystal clear, even to the visiting child's parents, but they seemed to brush it off. Maybe they were used to such antics; who knows?

Feeling a bit awkward about the whole situation, I mustered up the courage to ask them to intervene. Unfortunately, their child wasn't in the mood to listen. That's when I decided it was time for a change in strategy. I whispered to my son, telling him to ditch the "good host" act and stand up for himself – not quietly, but loud enough for the naughty child and his parents to hear.

Needless to say, the parents weren't thrilled, and the mischievous child probably didn't appreciate it either. But you know who did? My son. It was like a superhero moment for him, a confidence booster that echoed, "My dad's got my back, no matter what."

From that day forward, my son knew he could rely on his father for support. It wasn't just about that particular fight; it was about instilling the assurance that I'd always be there, ready to stand beside him. And in the grand narrative of raising twins, that moment became a pivotal plot twist, reinforcing the bond between a father and his child.

5. *Money – learning the economic value of goods:*

Teaching my twins about money became a sort of adventure, and it all started with our shopping escapades. Whether we were at a giant mall, a bustling supermarket, or dealing with a street vendor or an auto driver, I made sure the kids were there to witness my negotiating skills. Sometimes it was a bold move, and sometimes just a little trick with a street vendor.

Initially, they couldn't quite grasp why I bothered negotiating over a few rupees when it wouldn't make a big difference to us. That's when I explained the concept of fair economic value. It wasn't just about the money; it was about understanding the right price for a product or service. I wanted them to learn to distinguish between a fair deal and someone trying to take advantage.

To drive the point home, there were times I paid a bit more when the need was high, just to illustrate the concept. Conversely, when the situation allowed, we went all out on negotiating. I also took the chance to introduce them to the idea of impulse purchases in a retail store – the difference between needs wants, and desires.

While they might not be experts in the money game just yet, I'm thrilled that we started this learning process at the right age. I'm confident these skills will serve them well as they approach their teen years.

I feel reassured knowing that they're gradually becoming equipped to handle their pocket money responsibly. It's not just about the art of negotiation; it's about instilling a sense of financial awareness that will stay with them as they navigate the twists and turns of growing up.

The journey has just begun for them. They are on their journey to learn some of the essential aspects of life. By no means the above stories are the defining ones or the final ones, but I think they are the starting point and a narrative of so many stories that we live every day. These moments are helping them become more mature individuals and more conscious humans.

Weaving Moments into Memories

There's no handbook for being a perfect mother. It's a journey filled with ups and downs, trials and errors. My path was far from smooth, and I encountered my fair share of challenges. Failures became my greatest teacher, each setback a lesson that guided me toward a better understanding of what worked and what didn't.

Not every attempt was a success; many times, things didn't go as planned. But in those moments, I discovered the power of restarting. It's the reset button that allows you to tailor your approach to suit your child's unique needs. I've shared my tips and tricks, hoping they might work for others, but the real magic lies in the individualized journey with each unique child.

Throughout this rollercoaster of successes and failures, what stands out the most are the remarkable and cherishing memories. When my kids look back, I want them to remember smiles, joy, and a sense of strength.

In the end, it's not about being a perfect mother; it's about being a mother who embraced the journey, learned from it, and created a tapestry of memories that weaves through the laughter, tears, and triumphs.

This book is a heartfelt journey of a mother, acknowledging the imperfections and challenges of parenthood. As the final pages of this book unfold, let it stand as a tribute to the imperfect yet extraordinary journey of motherhood. May it serve as a reminder that in the tapestry of trials, failures, and restarts, we find the threads of love, joy, and strength that weave a story uniquely our own.

Here's to the remarkable memories, the lessons learned, and the smiles that linger as our children look back on a journey that was, in its imperfections, perfectly ours.

References

1. Klein, B. (2021, August). Insights on How to Parent Twins. *Psychology Today*. https://www.psychologytoday.com/us/blog/twin-dilemmas/202108/insights-how-parent-twins

2. Lewin, V., Friedman, J., & Segal, E. (n.d.). *New Understandings of Twin Relationships: From Harmony to Estrangement and Beyond*. Routledge. https://www.routledge.com/New-Understandings-of-Twin-Relationships-From-Harmony-to-Estrangement-and/Klein-Hart-Martinez/p/book/9780367228736

3. Twins Trust. (n.d.). *Twin Studies*. https://twinstrust.org/information/parenting/milestones-and-development/twin-studies.html

4. Friedman, J. A. (2014, September). The Psychology of Parenting Twins. *Psychology Today*. https://www.psychologytoday.com/us/blog/meaningful-you/201409/the-psychology-parenting-twins

5. McCulloch, J. (2021, November). Twins in the World: The Legends They Inspire and the Lives They Lead. *Psychology Today*. https://www.psychologytoday.com/us/blog/twofold/202111/literary-highlights-five-new-books-about-twins

6. Tinglof, C. B. (2007). *Parenting School-Age Twins and Multiples*. Sourcebooks.

7. Bowman, K. (2003). *Twins: A Practical Guide to Parenting Multiples from Conception to Preschool*. Ballantine Books.

8. Malmstrom, P. (2008). *The Art of Parenting Twins: The Unique Joys and Challenges of Raising Twins and Other Multiples*. Three Rivers Press.

9. Sonnenberg, V. (2016). *Parenting Twins: The Handbook for Containing Chaos and Preserving Memories in the First Year*. Ulysses Press.

10. Piontelli, A. (2002). *Twins: From Foetus to Child*. Routledge.